How to Build a Computer
(For Beginners)

By
John H. Gower III

ISBN: 978-1-257-86129-3 Second Edition Paperback
ISBN: 978-1-257-83890-5 First Edition Paperback
ISBN: 978-1-257-80305-7 Hard Cover
ISBN: 978-1463664060 Forth Edition Paperback

First Edition Published 2011

Table of Contents

Chapter 1
Gathering Information

So you want to build a computer? Well, first question you should ask yourself is what kind of performance you would like to receive out of it? Do you want a computer that can be capable of playing games on it? Or do you want just one you can browse the internet and do word documents on?

When you figure out what you're interested in doing with the computer, your first step is to gather information, what I mean by that is set your budget on how much you want to spend. If you don't have access to a computer, that has the internet, you can go to your local library to get internet access from one of their computers for free.

Go to google.com search for parts and start comparing prices that fits your budget. Now I suggest you get a paper and write down the parts you will need for pricing. If you are familiar with the AMD or Intel Processors, I recommend AMD because I worked with it a lot and it is a good company. On the following page area is a list of parts you will need to start pricing:

Note: *Page 6 shows a list of computer parts you need to build your computer. Write this down on a piece of paper with spaces in between.*

Computer Hardware:

- Video Card (Graphics Card)
- Motherboard
- Processor
- Memory
- Case
- Power Supply
- Hard Drive
- Monitor
- CD Rom Drive
- Keyboard and Mouse

Computer Software:

Microsoft Office 2007 Professional Operating System (Windows XP or Windows 7) I recommend XP because 7 are not compatible with some older computer parts.

Chapter 2
Buying the Parts

The first thing you should consider doing when buying the parts is to check how much you are willing to spend. Now for example, my budget is $1500.

The first thing you want to do is to price motherboards. I like the AMD processors so I am going to price motherboards that have the compatibility to support the processor AMD.

Sometimes places carry barebones which are cases with the power supply and sometimes motherboard is already in there. In our example we are going to buy a bare bone computer. I will show you some sites to check out on the next page.

You can purchase your computer parts either online or at a computer store. Here are some examples of great websites to go to:

- http://www.tigerdirect.com

- http://www.pricewatch.com

- http://www.softmartsurplus.com

It is very important to check the sockets *(referring on the motherboard)* because there are certain sockets that can fit the processor slot. That's only if you purchase the processor separately from the motherboard.

They sometimes come in bundles so if you're new to this I recommend you purchase the bundle package that comes with the processor.

Ok, I went to tirgerdirect.com. you want to purchase the Biostar N68S3B GeForce Barebones Kit - Biostar N68S3B

Motherboard, AMD Phenom II X4 805 CPU, CPU Fan, Patriot 8GB (2x 4GB) DDR3 RAM, Seagate 1TB HDD, 22x DVDRW, Thermaltake ATX Mid-Tower, 450-Watt PSU for $299.99. That comes with the case motherboard, processor and fan, memory, CD Rom drive and hard drive.

Barebones Example:

The Barebones Example above has the case the memory, processor, hard drive, CD Rom drive and motherboard all together.

Now you need the keyboard, monitor, operating system (Windows 7), and mouse.

Next purchase the monitor for $79.99. The, I-Inc iP-192ABB 19" Class Widescreen LCD Monitor the I-Inc iP-192ABB 19" Class Widescreen LCD Monitor delivers a crisp and pristene quality picture with 1440 x 900 pixels at a 16:10 aspect ratio.

With 16.7 million colors and 5ms response time, the I-Inc iP-192ABB 19" Class Widescreen LCD Monitor not only makes your images pop, it makes them come alive on screen.

Combine these traits with low energy consumption and the I-Inc iP-192ABB 19" Class Widescreen LCD Monitor sounds like the ideal match for your personal computer.

The Picture below shows what it looks like:

19" LCD Monitor:

Now you need to purchase the operating system. You want to get Windows 7 for it.

So I am going to go to tigerdirect.com and type in the search Windows 7. I am going to purchase Microsoft Windows 7 Home Premium Operating System Software – DVD for $99.99 on tigerdirect.com.

With Microsoft Windows 7 Home Premium Operating System Software, you'll get the best entertainment experience on your PC! Windows 7 Home Premium makes it easy to create a home network and share all of your favorite photos, videos, and music.

You can even watch, pause, and rewind TV or record it to watch whenever and wherever you want. For the best entertainment experience on your PC, choose Windows 7 Home Premium.

Next you want to purchase the mouse and keyboard. I am going to go to tirgerdirect.com and type in the search box keyboard and mouse combo.

I want to purchase the Logitech 920-002565 MK120 Keyboard and Mouse Combo - USB, Optical Mouse, 1000 DPI, Spill Resistant Design, and Black for $19.99.

In picture above are the Logitech 920-002565 MK120 Keyboard and Mouse Combo - USB, Optical Mouse, 1000 DPI, Spill Resistant Design, black.

Now if you want to purchase some extra software you can also. I do in my example, so I can do word documents.

I am going to go to, softmartsurplus.com and purchase the Microsoft Office 2007 Professional for only $170. Now I am finished.

Ok now once you have priced all the hardware and software that you need to build your computer. It doesn't have to be exactly the one I am doing.

But it's only an example. You can either purchase them online, or at a Computer Store near you.

Your next step is to wait till you receive the items either by, UPS or the shipping method you used.

Chapter 3
Getting the Right Tools Ready to Build

Now you need to get the tools ready to build. You can purchase a tool kit. That has all the tools you need for building your pc. Very cheap either online or at a computer store. It is very helpful and very handy. I recommend it. All professional computer people always carry these tools.

All tools are fully demagnetized to protect your computer's hard drive or magnetic media from damage and each tool is conveniently stored in a custom designed case. Tackles minor electronic maintenance jobs with ease. View example picture on the following page.

Belkin Professional Computer Service Tool Kit shown in the picture below:

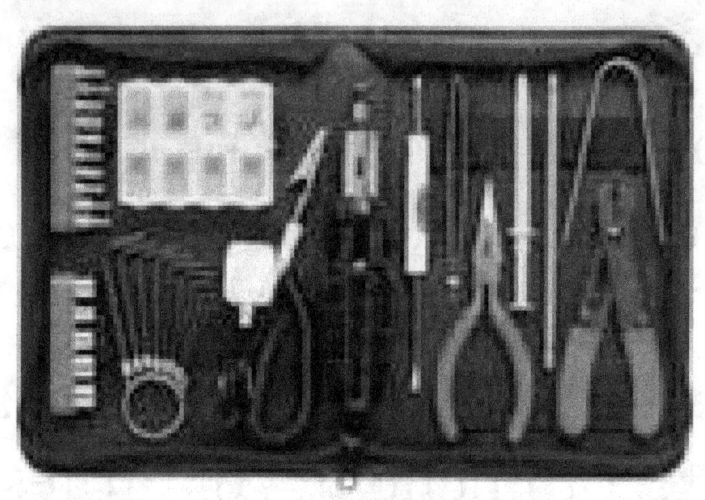

What I use is a Phillips screwdriver and a static band to ground myself from static electricity. That is all I use for building a computer, but it is recommended that you follow the proper procedures.

Now once you received your parts in the mail lay them out on a table which I will talk about in the next chapter.

Chapter 4
Prepare your area to build

Selecting the proper workspace for your computer building project is very important. You need enough space to layout all of your parts, and you need good lighting to see what you are doing inside the case.

A large computer desk is a good area to work on, where you can have the parts all to one side.

Another solution is a large kitchen table with overhead lights.

You want to avoid working on the ground, and especially the carpet because of the threat of static electricity. You will need to have an ESD wrist strap handy and use it at all times when handling your PC parts and building your computer.

Once you have selected your workspace, go ahead and layout all of your tools and parts. We are ready to get started building the PC!

Chapter 5
Building Steps

Now that we have our workspace ready to go with our parts and tools laid out, we need to get our case ready to install everything. Most cases are laid out generally the same way, but our example assumes that you are using a standard sized ATX type case. Some cases have a removable tray that the motherboard fits on also, but the holes to install the motherboard will be the same. If these directions don't match the type of case you have, make sure to consult the documentation that came with your case.

Please read the following steps carefully.

Step 1- Opening the Case

Open the left side of the case, by removing the two screws in the back that hold the side on. Once the screws are removed, you may need to slide the panel back completely along the rails to remove it. Your case may have clips instead of screws, and you will need to undo the clips to remove the side. If you have a more expensive case that is locking, make sure the lock is undone before trying to remove the side of the case.

Once you have access to the inside of the case, you will probably see some hardware that has been included, including instructions. You may want to go ahead and open the bag of hardware and have the instructions handy as you follow along.

(Now is probably the best time to get your wrist strap out and get yourself properly grounded to avoid damage to your parts as we start working. Follow the installation directions of your wrist strap and continue on below. If you choose to work without a wrist strap, make sure to touch the case every time you start working on the computer, to remove static electricity from your body.)

Step 2- Understanding the Inside of the Case

After taking a look inside the case for the first time, you should see a lot of wires running every which way. The twisted looking wires are used to connect such things are your case speaker, hard drive light, power light, and power switch.

There may be an extra set of wires running from the top or the bottom of the case as well that connect to the USB ports on the front of your case if it so equipped.

You may have a fan at the bottom front of the case with a power wire running from it, which is used for cooling and airflow. There should be a speaker mounted somewhere on the front part of the case with a wire coming from it that will later be attached to the motherboard.

If you bought a case that already has a power supply installed, you will see the power supply mounted in the upper rear, with many different power connectors coming out of it. These various connectors are used to supply power to your hard drive, CD/ROM and DVD drives, floppy drive, speaker, and motherboard etc.

We won't be doing anything with these wires until we get the motherboard installed, so move everything aside as good as you can, to make a clear open space to mount the motherboard into the case.

Step 3- Install Motherboard Standoffs

Now you will want to get that bag of hardware back out that came with your case, and remove the motherboard standoffs. You will probably also need to get your needle nose pliers ready for screwing them in. The motherboard standoffs are the small screws that have a male and female end to them. This will allow a base for your motherboard to set on, that you can then attach the screws to. Remove your motherboard from the case and packaging and examine the holes that are present on the motherboard. This is where the screws will go.

Examine the holes inside the case, and hold the motherboard inside the case, and figure out where you need to screw the standoffs into the case to match the holes on the motherboard. When you think you have them all in correctly, set the motherboard on top of the standoffs one last time to make sure you didn't miss any.

Make sure you get the standoffs screwed in tightly, as these will serve as the base and support for your motherboard on the case. You can now remove the motherboard, set it aside, and continue.

Step 4- Install I/O Plate

The I/O plate is the metallic looking piece that fits in the large rectangular space on the back of the case. It should snap into the space with ease, and it will fit around all of the I/O ports on the back of the motherboard when it is installed.

Step 5- Remove front Covers on Case

Now would also be a good time to figure out think about where you want to install your DVD/CD Rom drive and floppy drive at.

On the front of the case, you will see the individual panels that can be removed. Depending on the size of your case, you should have a few of the larger panels towards the top. Think about where you want the DVD/CD Rom to be installed, and pop out that section. For aesthetics, generally the top most slot works the best.

Repeat this process for the floppy drive if you bought one, and remove the smaller panel below where you want your floppy drive to sit at.

NOTE: You may need to use your flat head screwdriver to gently pry the panels loose. Don't put too much effort into it though, as they should easily come out.

When it comes time to install these drives, you will now be able to slide them in from the front of the case.

We have successfully prepared the case for installing parts, and now it is time to move on and install the power supply if your case did not come with one already.

If the case that you bought already has a power supply installed, then you can skip this step. If not continue on below.

Take the power supply out of the box and make sure to switch to 115v if it is not already (If you are outside the United States, this will be different)

Mount the power supply to the upper back part of the case by inserting the power supply through the side of the case, and then sliding it on the support rails in the back.

(NOTE: If your power supply has two fans, make sure the second fan is pointing down.)

If you have everything lined up correctly, you should be able to attach the power supply to the case with the four screws in the back that hold it in place.

We now have the power source necessary to run everything!

Step 6- Prepare motherboard for installation.

The next step is to prepare the motherboard for installation.

It may not even be necessary to do anything on this step, depending on the age and type of your motherboard.

Motherboards over time have lost many of the 'jumpers' that were required for configuring the board. Most of the setup is done with the BIOS (Basic Input Output System) that is accessible when you first turn on your computer.

You will need to view your motherboard instruction manual, and see if any jumpers need to be set on the motherboard itself for configuration.

Common settings include CPU voltage and bus speed, so read through the directions and make sure that these or anything else does not need to be configured on motherboard before continuing.

After you set anything on the motherboard that is necessary, you will want to lay out the number of screws you need to install the motherboard inside the case, and set the motherboard on a flat surface so we can install the CPU and memory. It is a good idea to keep the motherboard on the anti static bag that it came with to reduce the possibility of damage due to static.

We also recommend having the motherboard manual handy as we start to build your computer.

Let's move on to installing the CPU and heat sink next!

Step 7- Inspect the CPU

Before installing the CPU, we recommend that you take it out of the packaging and verify that you have received the correct one that you ordered. With all of the different core types and speeds, it is necessary to check before installing. You also want to check the pins on the underside of the processor, and make sure that all are straight with no damage. Try to avoid touching the pins with your bare fingers if possible. If everything looks good continue on.

Step 8- CPU Installation

Depending on your choice of Intel or AMD, your socket type may look different. Generally, all sockets on a motherboard have a latching feature, which holds the CPU in place.

NOTE: If these instructions do not match your motherboard and CPU type then consult the directions that came with your CPU for proper installation.

Unlatch the socket on the motherboard by pulling the lever up.

You should see a small triangle on one corner of the socket. You will need to match this up to the triangle on the processor, so the triangles are oriented and in the same position. Once you have these lined up, simply set the CPU onto the socket and gently move until it falls into place.

(You shouldn't have to force the CPU in the socket, and if it is not going in easily, something is wrong. Check the pins for damage if it is not sliding in correctly)

Push the lever back down to secure the CPU into the socket.

Step 9- Heat sink/Fan Installation

Processors run very hot, and it is necessary to attach a cooling device to control the temperature as your computer runs. If you bought the retail version of your CPU selection like we recommended, it should have come with a fan and heat sink combo. Again, depending on your choice between AMD and Intel, your heat sink and fan may look different. We recommend following the directions that came with your CPU for specifics on attaching to the top of the CPU, but here are the general directions.

Remove the heat sink/fan from the box, and make sure to remove the plastic cover that is over the bottom. This plastic cover is to keep the thermal grease in place with shipment. You need to remove the plastic cover so the thermal grease can attach to the CPU and improve heat transfer.

Place the heat sink and fan combo squarely on the CPU.

Attach the mounting brackets from the heat sink over the tabbed parts of your CPU socket. Many times this is a small square tab sticking out on each side of the socket. It will probably be necessary to use a flat screwdriver to push down when attaching the second side.

There may be a large lever that you need to turn clockwise and push down to finish attaching the heat sink. This insures the heat sink and fan are firmly attached.

Step 10- Connect CPU Fan to Motherboard

Your motherboard should have a place to connect the wire from the CPU fan to, and it should match the number of pins that the connector has. Please consult your motherboard manual to see where you need to connect your CPU fan to for power. This is an important step, because we do not want to run the computer without proper cooling to the CPU, as it may cause damage.

We have just installed the Processor and are ready to continue building your new computer. The next step in the process is memory installation.

The next step is to get the memory installed and this is a very easy step.

1. Remove the memory from the packaging and notice the number of pins on the bottom of the memory module. One side will have more pins than the other side, and there will be a large gap in between the two sides of pins.

2. Look at the memory slots on the motherboard and you can see the same pattern, with one side having more pins than the other.

3. Make sure you match the pattern up on both the memory stick and the

motherboard, and place the memory into the slot, and firmly push down.

4.   The memory should 'snap' into place, and you want to make sure that the plastic tabs at each end of the memory slot are tightly secure to the sides of the memory.

5.   If you have more than one memory module, repeat the above process to install the remainder of the memory.

NOTE: You should not have to really force the memory into the slot, it should go fairly easily. Make sure you have the memory turned the right way, and that the side tabs are not in your way as you push it into the slot.

That was easy huh? Now that we have the 'core' of our components installed on the motherboard, it is time to install the motherboard itself. We installed the CPU and memory before installing the motherboard because it is generally easier to work with the motherboard out of the case. You could however install these things while the motherboard was in the case.

Since we have already prepared the case, installing the motherboard into the case should be fairly easy.

Step 11- Mount the Motherboard onto the Standoffs

1.   Put the motherboard into the case, and set it onto the open screw holes which have been created by the standoffs. If you matched the pattern before to the case, you should have the same number of openings to insert screws into. (To get the holes to line

up perfectly, you may need to push the motherboard back towards where the I/O plate is, as this generally fits snugly)

2.   Insert screws into all of the holes and tighten gently. It is not necessary to over tighten these screws.

You should now be looking at your motherboard installed inside the case! The I/O ports should be sticking out the back and should fit squarely and snug. If you could not install all of the screws or the I/O ports do not fit correctly through the plate, make sure to correct this before you continue. The slots on the motherboard to line up correctly and be straight for add on cards to be easily installed.

We have the motherboard installed, and now it is time to get all of the cables on the inside connected.

With the motherboard installed, it is time to connect the internal cables that run from the case.

Step 12- Connect the Cables from the Case

It is difficult to give detailed instructions for this, because every motherboard and case is different. In general, you should have twisted cables for the speaker, case fan, hard drive light, power light, power switch and reset buttons. You may also have cables for USB ports if your case has them built in.

Your motherboard manual will have a detailed diagram on where to attach these. Follow the directions on where these go for a smooth installation. Make sure to attach the wires in the correct orientation, usually each set of wires has a ground so it is pretty easy to figure out which way they go.

If you are not using onboard video via the motherboard, then the next step is to install the video card into the proper slot.

If you bought the video card separately and plan on installing a separate video card for your new computer, please continue below. If you bought a motherboard that has onboard video built in, you may skip this step.

Remove the card from the original packaging and look at the slot type on the card. It should match the slot that is on your motherboard. **(AGP and**

PCI Express are currently the most popular video card types)

Hold the card in the proximity of where it will be installed in the slot. You will need to remove the back cover plate with your screwdriver where the card will stick through the back of the case.

Gently install the card into the slot, by pushing until it fits snug into place. There may be an extra tab as part of the slot the wraps around and helps secure the card.

Replace the screw that you removed for the slot, to secure the card to the back of the case.

That is it for the video card installation, not too difficult is it? Next we need to attach the power supply connector(s) to our motherboard. In

This Case we are going to use the on board AGP.

This is a very quick step, and will allow us to prepare ourselves for a test to see how smoothly our computer building project is going.

Step 13- Attach the Power Supply Connector

If you have an ATX style power supply, it will have one large connector, and possibly a smaller square connector that both need to be attached to provide power to the motherboard. They can only be attached on way, and each have a tab that needs to be pressed as you push them into their respective slots. You should here a 'click' and be able to feel when they are secure.

With the CPU, memory, and video card installed on the motherboard, and our case cables and power supply connected, now is a good time to do a quick power up test to see if we get video or not, and to make sure that the fans are all operating correctly.

1.   Plug in your power strip to the wall and turn it on, and then plug the PC power cable that came with your motherboard or power supply from the surge strip to the back of the power supply. Make sure the power supply is set to the proper voltage (115v in the US) and that the switch is in the on position.

2.   A small LED light may come on somewhere on the motherboard, telling you that the motherboard now

has power. Your motherboard may or may not have such a light.

3.   Plug the monitor and keyboard into their respective ports.

4.   Make sure your monitor is also plugged in to your power strip.

NOTE: Make sure you have the CPU fan connected to the proper place on the motherboard for power. Starting the computer without proper CPU cooling can cause damage to the processor, even if it does not run for very long.

Now comes the moment of truth. Go ahead and push the power button on the front of the case (it should be the largest button on the front) and see what happens.

If all is well, you should hear the power supply fan, CPU fan and case fan(s) start, and see some video on the monitor for the first time. Here we want to make sure that all fans are operating as they should, and that we have video. If we can see something on the monitor, then it is very likely that the CPU and memory are operating properly and that everything is installed OK.

If everything that was just mentioned happens, then shut off the computer and move on to the next step.

Step 14- Oh No, Nothing is Happening!

If the computer will not power on, then double check your power connections from the power supply to the motherboard and try again. Double check to make sure your power switch cable is installed correctly to the motherboard.

If you fail to see video then make sure your monitor is attached correctly. If you hear the fans starting but do not see any video make sure that you attached the second power connector from your power supply to the motherboard. It should be a smaller type connector.

If you are still having problems, reverse your steps and reinstall the memory and video card and CPU. If you cannot get the machine to power on at this point, and are sure everything is installed correctly, then it is likely that you have a defective component. You will know if the power supply is defective because the fan will not run when you power it on. Consult with who you bought your parts from for more assistance on troubleshooting and determining which part is defective.

The next step on how to build a computer is to install the hard drive.

Now that we know our main components are working after doing our quick power up test, we can finish building the computer. We are going to configure all of the drives, and install them in the case.

Step 15- Installing the Hard Drive

Remove the hard drive from its packaging/anti static bag. Select where you want to place the hard drive within the case, usually there are a couple of spots labeled 'HDD' where the hard drive is intended to go.

On the top of the hard drive, there should be a diagram telling you how to jumper the drive for installation.

If this is your only hard drive, and it is an SATA type drive, then you can set the drive as 'master'. Follow the diagram and place the jumper across the pins to make this setting. Many times leaving a jumper off completely will default the drive as master.

If you are installing an IDE type drive with another IDE hard drive or DVD/CD rom drive on the same cable, then set your jumper for master or cable select. Cable select means the computer will auto configure it for you. If you do set the drive to master, make sure you set the other drive you are installing on the same cable to 'slave' by setting the jumper correctly.

Once you have the drive jumper and setup correctly, push it into the slot you want and line up the screw holes with the case. Make sure to leave the back to attach connections open, so you will want this facing to the rear.

Attach the four screws to the case and you are set!

Now we are on to installing the hard CD ROM drives.

Step 16- Installing the **CD ROM Drives**

When we prepared the case before, we recommended that you remove the front cover(s) for the location where you wanted to install your CD-Rom and/or DVD drive. The next step is to make sure they are configured correctly, and position them in the case.

Remove the drive from its packaging/anti static bag.

Your drive should be an IDE type drive, and we will need to configure the drive, depending on if it is installed on its own cable or not. If the drive is on its own cable, and you have already installed an SATA hard drive, then set the jumper to master on the drive.

Like the hard drive we configured before, there should be a diagram somewhere on the drive, or labeled on the drive directly how to configure it as master. If the drive is sharing a cable with the hard drive, we recommend setting is as cable select if your IDE hard drive was set to cable select, or slave if the IDE hard drive has been set to master.

You should have already removed the front cover of where you want it to go, so and slide the drive into the case from the front.

Line up the holes with the drive and the case, and make sure the drive is flush with the front edge of the case.

Attach the screws to the case to secure the drive.

If you have more than one CD-Rom or DVD drive to install, repeat the exact same process as above.

Now that we have all of our drives secure in the case, it is time to hook everything up.

This is starting to look like a real computer isn't it? We are approaching the home stretch so hang in there. We have to attach the drives to our motherboard and power supply next. The cables you need to attach everything should have come with either your motherboard or individual drives, depending on if you bought the retail or OEM versions. Get the cables out as you will need them to install the drives.

Step 17- Connect Hard Drive Cables

If you bought an SATA hard drive, the cable going from the drive to the motherboard is very easy to install, as the connectors can only fit one way into the drive and motherboard connections. Connect one end to the hard drive, and the other connector to the hard drive, aligning the connectors properly. If you bought an IDE hard drive, more than likely the connectors are tabbed, and can only fit one way into the connection slots. To be sure, when connecting the IDE cable to the hard drive, you want the red stripe facing closest to the power connecter. This is also known as 'pin 1', and is always installed this way. Attach the other end of the cable to the motherboard by installing it into the slot. Make sure both connections are snug and tight.

Attach the SATA power connector from the power supply to the back of the hard drive if you have this drive type or one of the standard power connectors if you have an IDE version. (A standard power connector will be the same shape as the connection slot on your drive, long and rectangular in shape).

Step 18- Connect CD-Rom / DVD Drive Cables

As described previously in this chapter, on an IDE cable more than likely the connectors are tabbed, and can only fit one way into the connection slots. To be sure, when connecting the IDE cable to the hard drive, you want the red stripe facing closest to the power connecter. This is also known as 'pin 1', and is always installed this way. Attach the other end of the cable to the motherboard by installing it into the slot. Make sure both connections are snug and tight.

Attach a standard power connector from the power supply to the back of the drive. (A standard power connector will be the same shape as the connection slot on your drive, long and rectangular in shape).

All of our drives are now secure, connected and have a power source. We can now finishing connecting things to the outside of the case.

Now that everything is finished up on the inside of the machine, we need to connect all of our external devices such as the keyboard, mouse, and monitor.

If you still have the monitor connected from before on our quick power up test great! If not, go ahead and connect it to the video port on the video card now. If you have onboard video this will be mixed in with the other I/O ports on the back of the case, and if you installed it separately to a slot it will be farther down in the back.

Connect the keyboard, mouse, and speakers to the matching I/O ports on the back of the case. Many times these are color coded so it makes it easier to connect. They are also labeled next to the ports with a mouse symbol for mouse, keyboard for keyboard etc.

Depending on how you plan on connecting to the internet, either connect the phone line to your modem OR connect the network cable that runs from you cable modem, DSL modem, or wireless router to the network port on the back of your computer. It will be the port that looks similar to a phone jack, just slightly larger.

If you bought a scanner or printer, you can go ahead and connect it now, since Windows will detect and set the drivers for you when you run installation for the first time.

With everything attached to the inside and the outside of your new computer, we are ready to try and do a full boot test for the first time. Keep the side off the case so we can make sure everything is functioning properly, and troubleshoot if necessary. Now we are almost finished.

Chapter 6

Running the Computer

The goal of the first boot, is to test out all of our hardware and make sure that there are no problems before we get ready to install the operating system.

Now that everything is connected, go ahead and press the power button to start the machine up. Check and make sure that things are operating like on our previous quick power on test, mainly that the fans are working and we have video.

If the computer has been built correctly to this point, you should see a posting of the memory available and then a message stating that a first boot device or OS needs to be installed. Since we have nothing on the new hard drive, this is normal, and shows that the computer is properly seeing the hard drive.

Next we need to go into the BIOS and configure the DVD drive to be bootable for installation of Windows.

We will need to access the BIOS now on your computer, and this is usually accomplished by pressing and holding down the 'delete' key after you turn on your computer. Depending on your BIOS type, the key or keys you enter may be different. Please consult your motherboard manual on how to access the BIOS if it is not the delete key.

You will also need to follow the instructions in your motherboard manual for changing the first boot up device, and you need to set the first boot device to be your DVD drive.

Why, you may ask, do we change the computer to boot from the DVD drive?

The newest versions of Windows are on media that is bootable, and will start the installation process themselves, when you turn on the computer. When you have a hard drive with nothing on it, this is a quick and easy way to get your operating system installed.

We should not be too concerned with any of the other settings in the BIOS at this time. Later, after we have everything installed and working properly, we can come back to the BIOS to tweak some settings, but for now it is not necessary.

Let's get ready to install our operating system on the hard drive.

This step may not even be necessary, but we wanted to include it for reference. The newest versions of Windows, including Windows XP and Windows Vista, have a way to partition and format the hard drive during the installation process. If you plan on installing either of these versions of Windows on a new hard drive as a standard installation, then you do not have to do anything except specify how you want the drive setup during the install process. Skip the information below and continue on to the next step.

If you plan on installing multiple operating systems, or want the drive split up into separate sections or partitions, then you may want to so this before starting the install. Third party utilities are available to handle partitioning and formatting, some of which are free. This will need to be done to the hard drive prior to installing windows if you have a specific way you want to set the drive up. Make sure to use a compatible file type if you do your own partitioning, NTFS for Windows XP is recommended, and Windows Vista uses a newer version of NTFS so make sure your partition utility program will set the drive up to be ready for Vista if you are planning to install it.

We are going to assume that this is a standard Windows installation, and continue on to the next step. With your new installation of Windows, you have now completed building your first computer, and you are ready to start tweaking your system!

You have now just built your first computer!

Congratulations!

Chapter 7
Finalizing and Enjoying your new Computer

Now boot your computer up. Follow the steps that windows ask you when you boot into windows. Now if you don't have internet, call your local phone or cable company and purchase an internet service package deal. Let them come out and hook up the internet up. Connect you cable from the modem to the new computer you built.

Now you have the internet. Go to the start button on the computer, search for the Windows Update button. It should be in the programs tab. Run the Windows Updates. Follow each step. Let it run, and restart. Now you can enjoy your newly built computer.

To find out more about the author and his book. Go to his website, http://www.jghitech.webs.com.

The author will be coming out with new book 2013 called "How to Build a Website (For Beginners)".

For more details please visit the website jghitech.webs.com.

www.ingramcontent.com/pod-product-compliance
Lightning Source LLC
Chambersburg PA
CBHW081219170526
45165CB00009B/2878

* 9 7 8 1 4 6 3 6 6 4 0 6 0 *